WHY CAN'T I LIVE FOREVER?

By Vicki Cobb, with illustrations by Ted Enik

Why Doesn't the Earth Fall Up?
and other not such dumb questions about motion

Why Can't You Unscramble an Egg?
and other not such dumb questions about matter

Why Doesn't the Sun Burn Out?
and other not such dumb questions about energy

Also by Vicki Cobb

Gobs of Goo

Lots of Rot

This Place Is Cold

This Place Is Dry

This Place Is Wet

This Place is High

This Place Is Crowded

This Place Is Lonely

WHY CAN'T I LIVE FOREVER?

and other not such dumb questions about life

BY VICKI COBB

illustrated by Mena Dolobowsky

DUTTON   LODESTAR BOOKS   NEW YORK

for Richard
V.C.

to Ceil and Jack, from me
M.D.

Text copyright © 1997 by Vicki Cobb
Illustrations copyright © 1997 by Mena Dolobowsky

Library of Congress Cataloging-in-Publication Data

Cobb, Vicki,
   Why can't I live forever?: and other not such dumb questions about life / by Vicki Cobb; illustrated by Mena Dolobowsky.
      p.   cm.
   Includes index.
   Summary: Discusses the answers to such questions as: Why are plants green? What makes a living thing a living thing? Why can't we live forever?
   ISBN 0-525-67505-1 (alk. paper)
   1. Life (Biology)—Miscellanea—Juvenile literature.   2. Biology—Miscellanea—Juvenile literature.   [1. Life (Biology)   2. Biology.]
I. Dolobowsky, Mena, ill.   II. Title.
QH501.C625   1997
574—dc20   95-52657 CIP AC

Published in the United States by Lodestar Books,
an affiliate of Dutton Children's Books,
a division of Penguin Books USA Inc.,
375 Hudson Street, New York, New York 10014

Published simultaneously in Canada
by McClelland & Stewart, Toronto

Editor: Virginia Buckley

Printed in Hong Kong
First Edition   10 9 8 7 6 5 4 3 2 1

CONTENTS

What Makes a Living Thing a Living Thing?

What do you do that shows you're alive? One thing you do is think. But you don't have to think to be alive. Plants don't think, and earthworms don't have enough brains to do that. So life has to be described in other ways. Scientists have decided that there are certain activities a living thing, or *organism*, does. Here's what they say.

Motion. You can see an animal move from one place to another. But a plant is not capable of moving in the same way. Although all living things move, the kind of motion they share cannot be seen without a microscope. When you look at living material under a microscope, you can see fluid moving from one place to another. This fluid is called *cytoplasm*. Its motion shows that an organism is alive.

Responsiveness. All living things must be able to sense whether conditions are threatening their life or are favorable. All organisms need a certain amount of warmth, food, and water. Many organisms depend on oxygen for survival, although some use other gases that are poisonous to us. By sensing their surroundings, living things get what they need to survive and also avoid dangers.

Metabolism. A living organism is a very highly organized and complicated structure. It is made of a countless variety of molecules including *proteins, fats,* and *carbohydrates.* (A molecule is a group of atoms. An atom is the smallest unit of an element such as carbon, hydrogen, or oxygen.) Proteins are very large molecules that are the building blocks of muscle, bone, blood, and other tissues in your body. In addition, some proteins are enzymes—molecules that control all the chemical reactions in anything alive. Scientists chose the word protein (meaning "of first importance") because they realized that proteins are necessary for life. Fats and carbohydrates are simpler molecules than proteins. They are used for food storage, among other jobs.

In order to maintain such a high level of organization, an organism needs energy. It also needs new materials for growth and repair. The source of energy and building materials for ongoing life is food. *Metabolism* is the sum of all the chemical activity of an organism. The activities of metabolism include getting food, digesting the food, making and repairing cytoplasm, burning food for energy, and getting rid of wastes

Death occurs when metabolism can no longer be kept going.

Reproduction. If organisms did not reproduce, life could not continue. Every living thing on Earth comes from other living things. So how did the first living thing on Earth appear? Could original life have come from nonliving chemicals?

There have been lots of guesses about how life began, but the best guess is that it happened about three and a half billion years ago. Conditions on Earth at that time were very different from what they are now. There was no oxygen in the air. In fact, the atmosphere was made up of methane gas (which is used as a fuel today), ammonia gas, and water vapor. The gases in this primitive atmosphere reacted with one another to form complicated molecules that fell into the oceans, making a kind of rich soup. The molecules in the oceans somehow became organized into simple living things. These earliest organisms became the ancestors of all the life that exists on Earth today.

We know lichens are alive because they do all the things living things do. But don't waste your time watching them grow. Most grow a tenth of an inch a year. Lichens grow ten times more slowly in the Arctic than here, so a large patch there may be as much as four thousand years old.

LICHENS

LICHENS LIVE ALMOST FOREVER.

IN SEARCH OF LICHENS

What Is the Smallest Living Thing?

If the smallest living thing can't be seen with the naked eye, it couldn't be discovered until the microscope was invented. This was about four hundred years ago, when a Dutch spectacle maker, Zacharias Janssen, first put two lenses together to act as a magnifier.

In April of 1663, Robert Hooke, an English biologist, placed a very thin slice of cork under a microscope. He invited others to look at the tiny boxlike structures that made up the body of the plant. He called each little structure a *cell* because it reminded him of the tiny rooms in monasteries where monks lived.

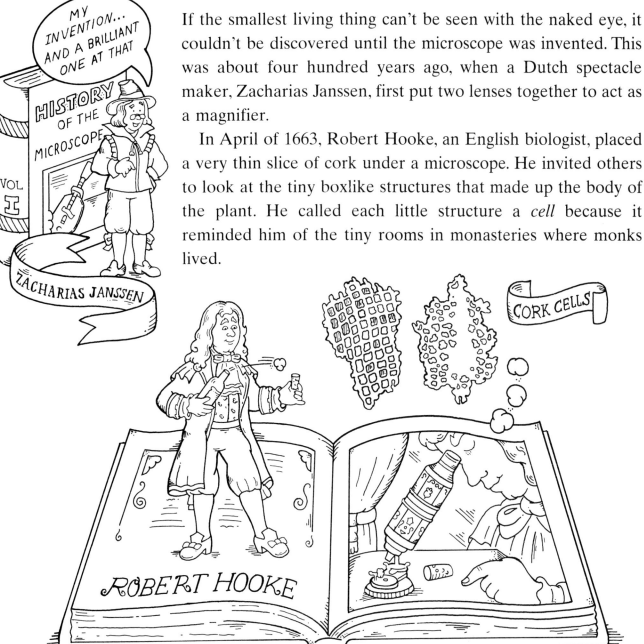

Not until almost two hundred years later did scientists discover that cells are important. After looking at different kinds of living things under the microscope, scientists realized that all living things are made of cells. The cell is the smallest unit of life. It performs all the previously listed activities that define life. Cells reproduce: All cells come from other cells. Each cell in a multicelled organism, like a human, metabolizes, responds to its surroundings, and has moving cytoplasm.

14

Single-celled organisms are the smallest living things. Algae are one-celled plants. Some kinds of algae form a scum on the surface of ponds. Protozoa are one-celled animals you can find in a drop of pond water and other watery habitats. Bacteria are single cells that live off other organisms both living and dead. The smallest one-celled organism is a bacterium that causes pneumonia. The largest single cell is an eight-inch ostrich egg.

Viruses are even smaller than bacteria. But some scientists argue that they are not true organisms because they can only reproduce themselves when they have invaded other cells. In other words, viruses are only "alive" when they are inside other living organisms.

Multicelled plants and animals are made up of many different kinds of cells that do specific jobs. You have skin cells, blood cells, muscle cells, bone cells, nerve cells, and lots more. Scientists have asked many questions about cells, such as "What do cells look like? How do they do their jobs?"

When Robert Hooke first saw the cork cells, he was looking at the *cell walls* of dead plant cells that contained no cytoplasm. You can see the living cells of an onion with an inexpensive magnifier. Some have a light in them and magnify thirty times actual size. With a pair of tweezers, pull off the thin skin on the inside surface of an onion layer. Place a tiny piece of the skin on a white surface. You can make out the cell walls through your magnifier. The cell walls are lined with a thin *cell membrane* that you can't see with your magnifier. You can also see a small, round, membrane-enclosed body in the center of each cell. This is called the *nucleus*. All plant cells have cell walls in addition to a cell membrane. Animal cells do not have cell walls. They are enclosed only by a thin cell membrane.

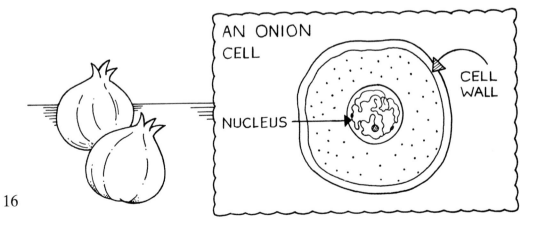

AN ONION CELL

NUCLEUS

CELL WALL

The largest organism in the world is a multicelled fungus that grows under the forest floor in Michigan. It covers more than thirty acres, weighs about a hundred tons, and could be up to ten thousand years old. So it is possible that the largest living thing is a kind of mushroom. It could also be the oldest.

Why Are Plants Green?

Questions that begin with "why" are often too hard for scientists to answer. They prefer questions they can answer by doing experiments. "What are the activities of green plants that keep them alive?" is the kind of question scientists like. The beginning of the answer to this question was discovered in the eighteenth century by Joseph Priestley, an English scientist. Priestley learned that, during the day, green plants take up carbon dioxide from the air and give off oxygen. When we breathe, we do just the opposite: We take up oxygen and give off carbon dioxide. Plants act like us at night, when there is no light.

19

EXPERIMENT!

1. GRIND SPINACH WITH SAND.

2. ADD ALCOHOL.

3. STRAIN.

VOILÀ... CHLOROPHYLL!

Another question scientists asked was, "What is the green stuff in plants and can we get it out?" Back in 1817, two French scientists extracted the pigment that makes plants green. They called it *chlorophyll* from two Greek words meaning "green leaf." They removed the chlorophyll by grinding up spinach with sand and mixing it with alcohol. Then they filtered the ground-up leaves and sand, keeping the liquid. With the help of an adult, you can also do this. Chop spinach in a food processor or blender. Add rubbing alcohol to extract the chlorophyll. Strain the mixture, keeping the liquid. Try other green plants, such as romaine lettuce or carrot tops. See if the greens are all the same color or slightly different.

Many scientists experimented to find out just how plants make food. They figured out that plants use water from the soil, carbon dioxide from the air, and energy from sunlight to make sugar, a basic food and the simplest carbohydrate.

water + carbon dioxide ⟶ sugar + oxygen

They called this process *photosynthesis,* which means "putting together with light." So green plants do two very important things: They make food from simple substances, and they replace the oxygen in the air.

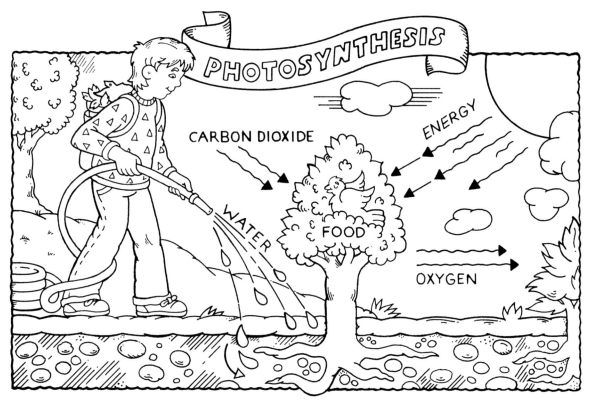

But how does chlorophyll fit into photosynthesis? Here are some of the things scientists have learned.

With a few exceptions, only green plants make food. Fungi use food made by green plants.

A leaf that is green and white only makes food where the green parts are.

A green plant that's kept in the dark for several days stops making food.

So they concluded that chlorophyll makes photosynthesis possible. Its job is to capture the energy of light. This energy is then used by plant cells to manufacture food. Since green plants make food, other organisms must either eat green plants or eat living things that eat green plants. Green plants are at the bottom of a chain of food. Without green plants, all other kinds of living things would not exist.

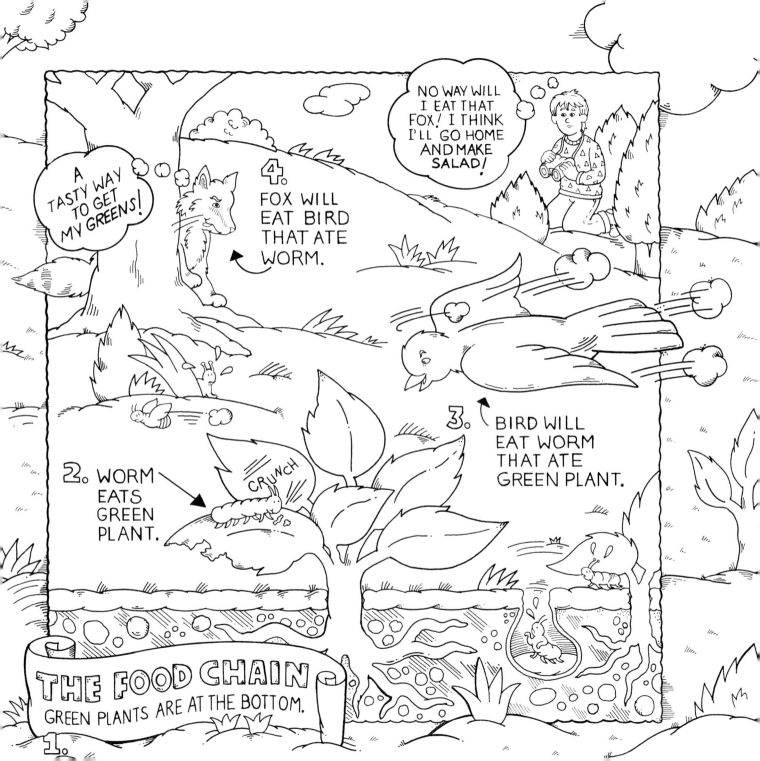

Why Is Blood Red?

Ever notice that hamburger is sometimes bright red and sometimes dark red? You can do an experiment to show how this happens. Open a package of fresh hamburger meat. The outside should be bright red. Break off a piece. Look at the color of the inside meat. If it has been ground recently, it will also be bright red. But if it has been in the package for a while, it will be dark red. Expose the dark red meat to the air for about a half hour. Does it change color? Something in the meat combines with oxygen in the air, changing its color to bright red.

25

Blood in your body is dark red in your veins and bright red in your arteries. Do you know why this is so? Bright red blood contains oxygen, which you take into your lungs when you breathe. Arteries deliver oxygen-rich blood to all parts of your body. Veins return oxygen-poor blood to the heart, which pumps it to the lungs to pick up another load. Oxygen is actually carried by a red pigment, called *hemoglobin,* that is inside red blood cells. Each hemoglobin molecule has an atom of iron, which combines with oxygen to make the blood bright red. (When iron metal rusts, it combines with oxygen in the air and becomes a reddish color.)

Fire is a chemical reaction that releases heat and light energy when oxygen combines with a fuel such as wood or oil. Fats and carbohydrates in your cells act as fuel for oxygen from your blood. But instead of giving off energy all at once, like a fire, your cells release energy for metabolism slowly, without burning you up. This slow release of energy is controlled by enzymes. There are thousands of different kinds of enzymes, and each has a particular job to do.

You can see a blood enzyme, called *catalase,* in action. You will need about a tablespoon of bright red, fresh hamburger meat and some hydrogen peroxide solution. (Hydrogen peroxide is available in the first aid section of any drugstore.) Fill half of a small glass with the hydrogen peroxide. Hold the glass up to the light. Can you see tiny bubbles in the liquid? Put the meat into the glass. Watch what happens to the bubbles.

Normally hydrogen peroxide slowly breaks down into oxygen and water. You see the tiny oxygen bubbles rising to the surface. Catalase in the blood of the meat speeds up this reaction, creating a foam. When you put hydrogen peroxide on a cut, the same foam forms because of your blood catalase. Cuts get infected if germs that don't like oxygen are allowed to grow. By flooding a wound with oxygen, you make it harder for these germs to survive.

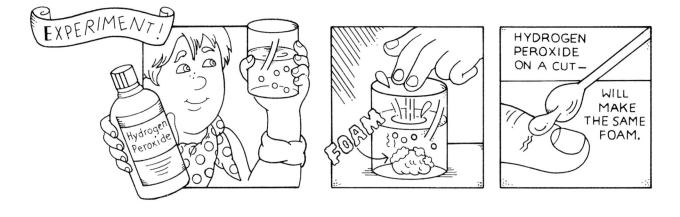

How Are All Living Things Alike?

If you look at fresh, living cells under the microscope, the nucleus is sometimes hard to see. The cells and all their parts are almost transparent. In the 1870s, a German scientist named Walther Flemming added a chemical dye to the cells under his microscope. He noticed that the nucleus took up more dye than the cell body. So he called the material in the nucleus *chromatin,* from a Greek word meaning "color."

Flemming dyed cells from some rapidly growing animal tissue. Cells grow by repeatedly dividing in two. He discovered that the dye killed the cells at different stages of division. It was like looking at jumbled still photos of a movie. With careful study, he figured out the order of the pictures so he understood the sequence of cell division. First the chromatin suddenly gets organized into a string of oddly shaped beads. These beadlike structures are called *chromosomes,* which means "colored bodies." Chromosomes have the amazing ability to construct exact copies of themselves using small molecules found in cytoplasm. Each step in the copying process is controlled by enzymes. In this way, they double their number just before a cell divides in two. After cell division, each new cell contains a full set of chromosomes. All cells have chromosomes, but you can only see them when dividing cells have been dyed.

A CELL DIVIDING

CHROMOSOMES

MY MEMOIRS

Chemical DYE

WALTHER FLEMMING

What are chromosomes made of? What do they do inside a cell? These questions kept scientists busy for more than a hundred years after Flemming. This is what they discovered. All living things have chromosomes in their cell nuclei. Chromosomes are made up of extremely large molecules with a very long name—deoxyribonucleic acid—or DNA, for short. If you could stretch out a DNA molecule, it would look like a ladder that has been twisted into a spiral. A *gene* is a section of DNA along a chromosome. Each gene is a master plan that tells the cell how to make a particular protein, including enzymes. Since proteins are the most important molecules, it's fair to say that any organism is the result of all its proteins. So the sum of all the genes equals the total plan for an individual.

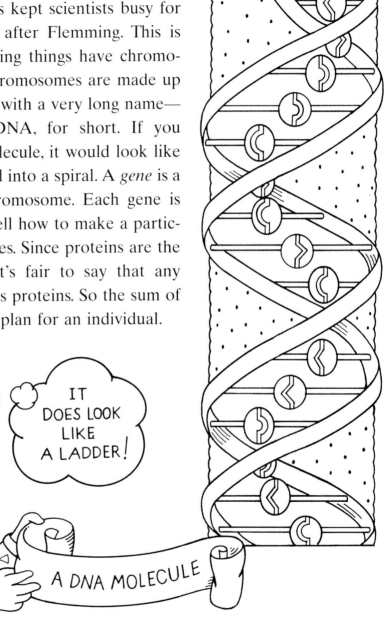

30

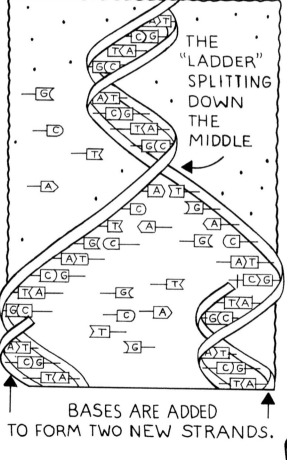

THE "LADDER" SPLITTING DOWN THE MIDDLE

BASES ARE ADDED TO FORM TWO NEW STRANDS.

How can DNA hold the plans for the tens of thousands of proteins that make up an organism? It turns out that DNA, the information molecule, is actually a code. The rungs of a DNA ladder are made up of two different linked pairs of distinctive groups of atoms known by the initials *A, T, C,* and *G. A* always pairs with *T,* and *C* always pairs with *G.* The order of the pairs is the genetic code that is the plan for a protein. How many different combinations can these two pairs make? Enough to make genetic codes for every characteristic of every living thing on Earth. Amazingly, all organisms, even most viruses, contain DNA.

DNA copies itself when a cell divides. The DNA molecule unzips down its middle, leaving each side of the ladder with a string of half the *A-T* or *C-G* pair. Each string then serves as a model to construct its opposite according to the code. For example, a string that is *A-T-T-G-C* will construct a string that is *T-A-A-C-G.* In this way, the genes pass on information to the next generation of cells.

DNA COPYING ITSELF

What Makes a Pea Plant a Pea Plant, a Fruit Fly a Fruit Fly, and a Person a Person?

A pea plant has fourteen chromosomes, a fruit fly has eight, and a person has forty-six. Chromosomes come in pairs, and every kind of living thing has its own number. So a pea plant has seven pairs, a fruit fly has four, and we have twenty-three. Since chromosomes are made of DNA, it's clear that we have a lot more DNA than either pea plants or fruit flies have. This makes sense. Humans are a lot more complicated than plants or flies. If we could unravel all the DNA in one of our cells, it would have a length of about six feet. We need many genes, more than one hundred thousand, to pass on information. One difference between a pea plant, a fruit fly, and a person is that each has its own set of genes.

Think of it this way: The DNA genetic code is like the letters of the alphabet. The DNA for each *species,* or kind of living thing, is like a language. Human DNA is a different language than plant DNA or animal DNA. Our DNA tells cells to manufacture the kinds of protein molecules that make us human. It also has the information that decides the color of our eyes, how tall we'll be, and whether we are male or female. You might think of each person as a separate book. We're all written in the same language, but the details of our stories are different.

Scientists are very familiar with the twenty-three pairs of human chromosomes. They can tell from the chromosomes whether a cell came from a male or a female or if a baby has a certain birth defect, such as mental retardation. They have also located specific genes on chromosomes—they know their address. A huge project, involving many countries and thousands of scientists, is underway to map all of the more than one hundred thousand human genes. Scientists hope that someday this information will give clues to many diseases and to the traits we inherit from our parents. Recently scientists have cracked the code of every gene in a bacterium that causes flu in people. It has 1,723 genes with almost two million *A-T* and *G-C* pairs. Understanding how this relatively simple cell lives can shed light on other cells, including human ones.

Why Can't I Live Forever?

We all understand the human life cycle: We are born, we grow up, we have children, we grow old and die. But the simplest living things, which are only one cell, are different. Instead of growing old and dying, they split and become two cells, called *daughter cells*. Then the two daughter cells become four, four become eight, and so on. Each daughter cell has exactly the same DNA as the cell it came from. This kind of cell division is a form of asexual *reproduction* because there is only one parent. One-celled organisms can die if they are eaten or suddenly have no water or food. But in their life cycle, they don't die—they reproduce. Many cells in our bodies reproduce like these single-celled organisms. The DNA in each kind of cell—muscle cell, skin cell, nerve cell—never changes in the daughter cells. Since you were originally a single cell, and all your cells came from that cell, all your cells have exactly the same DNA.

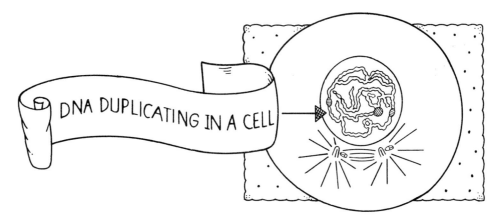

DNA DUPLICATING IN A CELL

More complicated living things, like people, reproduce by *sexual reproduction.* You began when a sperm cell from your father united with an egg cell from your mother. Sperm and egg cells are different from other human cells in a very important way: They each have only twenty-three chromosomes—half a complete set and half the DNA needed to make a person. When a sperm enters an egg, the complete number is restored. So you got half your chromosomes from your father and half from your mother.

The twenty-three pairs of chromosomes are like cards in a deck. When eggs and sperms are formed in your parents' bodies, each pair is split as if the deck was shuffled. Your brothers and sisters get a different mixture or "hand" than you do. You share *some* but not all of the chromosomes present in other members of your family. The only people who share exactly the same DNA are identical twins. They are two individuals who developed from a single fertilized egg that became two separate cells. Each cell then became a person.

You might want to make a family tree to show where some trait, like a dimple or eye color, got passed on from one person to another. The entire family might have fun choosing which trait to follow.

Shuffling DNA creates many kinds of people. This shuffling ensures that the strongest will survive to reproduce. The human race can keep getting stronger. Individuals die. But DNA can get passed along for generations to come.

How Long Can We Live?

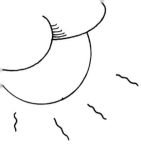

Jeanne Calment of France recently celebrated her 121st birthday. How is she doing? She doesn't hear very well, she can't walk, and she can't see. But she thinks that's normal for her age. Twenty years ago, when she was 100, she was still riding her bicycle around town. Most people can expect to live about seventy-five to eighty-five years. If we could keep our bodies as fresh and new as they are at two years old, we could easily last a hundred years.

Scientists have wondered about how long we can live. They have grown human cells in the laboratory. These cells die after about seventy cell divisions. What causes this? Is there a gene that acts like a clock? We don't know. Some cells in our body live longer than others. We don't know why. Are there genes that protect the cells of the body? If we discovered them, could we someday eliminate disease as a cause of death? No one knows. We know that living a long time is inherited and that our body parts wear out as we age, just like an old car. Jeanne Calment's mother lived to eighty-six and her father lived to ninety-three. Obviously her body parts have the genes to make them last. But we don't know how.

What is the ideal way to die at the end of a long life? We aren't really sure, but we think that a person can stay healthy and active until the day he or she dies. Death is a natural part of the life process.

SCIENTIFIC TERMS

asexual reproduction A method of reproduction that involves only one parent. Simple one-celled plants and animals divide in half producing two daughter cells. Cells in multicelled organisms reproduce this way when tissues grow.

carbohydrates Sugar and starch molecules manufactured by plants in the process of photosynthesis. They serve as the bottom of the food chain and are the food source for all animals and plants.

catalase A blood enzyme that helps break down hydrogen peroxide into water and oxygen.

cell The basic unit of life. All living things, from one-celled bacteria to multicelled humans, are made of cells.

cell membrane The thin skin that encloses the cell.

cell wall The semi-rigid nonliving structure that is outside the cell membrane of a plant.

chlorophyll A green plant pigment that absorbs energy from the sun. It enables plants to make sugar from carbon dioxide and water.

chromatin The material in the nucleus of cells that picks up a chemical dye and becomes colored under the microscope. Chromatin is organized into chromosomes during cell division.

chromosomes The tiny bodies in the cell nucleus that become visible during cell division. Chromosomes are made up of DNA. In sperm and egg cells chromosomes carry the hereditary information that is passed on to offspring.

cytoplasm The living material of cells.

daughter cells The two cells produced by asexual reproduction (cell division).

DNA Short for deoxyribonucleic acid, long threadlike molecules that contain the genetic codes needed for life. All organisms have DNA.

enzymes Proteins that control all the chemical reactions of living things.

fats Molecules made by living things from carbohydrates; energy-rich food stored within the organism.

gene A section of DNA along a chromosome. Each gene is a master plan for making one protein. Each gene controls some specific trait that is passed on to future generations.

hemoglobin The red pigment in blood. It is responsible for carrying oxygen to all the cells of the body.

metabolism All of the chemical reactions of an organism that keep it alive. An organism is constantly taking in molecules from the environment and giving off waste. The activities of metabolism include getting food, digesting the food, making and repairing cytoplasm, burning food for energy, and getting rid of wastes.

nucleus (nuclei, plural) The membrane-enclosed body in the center of a cell. It contains the DNA that directs all the activities of the cell.

organism Any independent living thing, plant, or animal.

photosynthesis The process by which green plants manufacture sugar, using water, carbon dioxide, and energy from the sun.

proteins Large, complicated molecules that are essential for life. The living material of organisms is mostly protein.

sexual reproduction Reproduction that involves two parents. A new individual begins when a sperm cell and an egg cell unite.

species A kind of plant or animal. Human beings are a species. Dogs are a different species.

Index